50 Decadent Shortbread Recipes

By
Brenda Van Niekerk

Copyright © 2012 Brenda Van Niekerk
All rights reserved.

ISBN-13:978-1502383341
ISBN-10: 1502383349

Table Of Contents

Creamy Shortbread Biscuits 7
Scotch Shortbread Balls 8
Pecan Shortbread 9
American Shortbread 10
Orange And Saffron Shortbread 11
Fruit Mincemeat Shortbread 12
Shortbread Made With Rolled Oats 13
Health Shortbread 14
Party Shortbread 15
Scotch Shortbread 16
Shortbread 17
Petticoat Tails 18
Millionaires Shortbread 19
Butterscotch Shortbread 21
Ginger Shortbread 22
Cheddar Shortbread 23
Chocolate Shortbread 25
Chocolate Chip Shortbread 26
Chocolate Dipped Shortbread 27
Lavender Shortbread 28
Honey Shortbread 29
Coconut Shortbread 30
Lemongrass Shortbread 31
Cinnamon Shortbread 32
Rum And Raisin Shortbread 33
Traditional Scottish Shortbread 34
Whisky Chocolate Chip Shortbread 35
Whisky Pistachio Shortbread 36

- Lemon Almond Shortbread...37
- White Chocolate And Macadamia Nut Shortbread...38
- Maple And Walnut Shortbread...39
- Rosemary And Walnut Shortbread...40
- White Chocolate And Cherry Shortbread...41
- Lemon Verbena Shortbread...42
- Espresso And Dark Chocolate Shortbread...43
- Mocha Shortbread...44
- Cranberry Brandy Shortbread...45
- Lemon Honey Shortbread...46
- Chai Shortbread...48
- Nougat Shortbread...49
- Chocolate Rose Shortbread...50
- Blue Cheese And Fig Shortbread...51
- Fig And Ginger Shortbread...52
- Chili Chocolate Shortbread...53
- Strawberry And Cracked Black Pepper Shortbread...54
- Pecan And Cranberry Chocolate Shortbread...55
- Amaretto And Cherry Shortbread...56
- Vanilla And Saffron Shortbread...57
- Cardamom And Rose Shortbread...58
- Cardamom And Pistachio Shortbread...59
- Apricot And Walnut Shortbread...60
- Coffee Liqueur And Hazelnut Shortbread...61

Creamy Shortbread Biscuits

Ingredients

    500 ml flour
    245 ml margarine
    190 ml icing sugar
    125 ml corn flour

Method

Beat the margarine and icing sugar until creamy.

Beat in the flour and corn flour.

Drop teaspoons onto a greased baking tray.

Bake at 160 degrees C until lightly brown.

Scotch Shortbread Balls

Ingredients

    250 ml butter
    125 ml brown sugar
    625 ml flour

Method

Mix the butter and sugar together.

Beat in the flour and mix thoroughly.

Chill the dough.

Shape into 2.5 cm balls and place on an un-greased baking sheet.

Press a criss-cross design on top of each ball with a floured fork.

Bake at 150 degree C for 20 minutes. The tops should not be brown.

Pecan Shortbread

Ingredients

160 ml icing sugar
245 ml butter
5 ml vanilla essence
500 ml flour
250 ml pecan nuts

Method

Mix all the ingredients together (except for the pecan nuts).

Roll out to a 9mm thickness, cut with 3 cm round cutter.

Place on a baking sheet.

Bake at 160 degrees C until starting to brown (do not allow to brown).

Decorate with pecan nuts.

American Shortbread

Ingredients

100 g margarine
125 ml sugar
1 egg
300 g flour
5 ml baking powder

Crust

25 g margarine
1 egg
250 g sugar
150 g desiccated coconut
25 ml apricot jam

Method

Cream the margarine and sugar.
Add the unbeaten egg.
Add flour and baking powder.
Press dough into greased baking tin, 21 cm by 34 cm.
Mix crust ingredients (except jam) together.
Spread the jam over the dough.
Crumble coconut mixture over jam.
Bake at 180 degrees C for 30 minutes.
Cut into squares while still warm.

Orange And Saffron Shortbread

Ingredients

230 g margarine
25 ml sugar
10 ml grated orange rind
500 ml flour
5 ml saffron

Method

Beat margarine until creamy.

Add the sugar and grated rind.

Stir in the flour and saffron.

Place mixture in a piping bag fitted with a rosette tube.

Place piped rosettes onto a greased baking sheet.

Bake at 180 degrees C for 20 minutes.

Fruit Mincemeat Shortbread

Ingredients

315 ml flour
120 ml margarine
50 g castor sugar
60 ml fruit mincemeat

Method

Cream the margarine and sugar together.

Add the flour and fruit mincemeat into the margarine mixture.

Mix well together.

Press into a greased round 20 cm cake pan.

Decorate the edge with a fork and cut into 8 segments.

Prick all over.

Bake at 170 degrees C for 40 minutes.

Cut into segments again.

Sprinkle with castor sugar before cooling.

Shortbread Made With Rolled Oats

Ingredients

    130 ml sugar
    130 ml butter
    240 g rolled oats

Method

Heat sugar and butter until melted.

Add the rolled oats and mix well.

Put into 2 greased sandwich tins; beat down well with the back of a spoon.

Back at 160 degrees C until a light biscuit color.

Let cool in tins.

Health Shortbread

Ingredients

975 ml flour
450 g butter
25 ml corn flour
Pinch salt
150 ml castor sugar
62,5 ml Ovaltine

Method

Rub the butter into the flour.

Add the Ovaltine and sugar.

Lastly add the corn flour and salt.

Press into a greased baking tin and pierce with a fork.

Bake for 1 hour in a 130 degree C oven.

When shortbread is cool, cut into fingers.

Party Shortbread

Ingredients

75 ml butter
37,5 ml castor sugar
375 ml flour
Pinch salt
Blanched almonds

Method

Cream the butter and sugar together.

Knead in the flour and salt.

Press into a greased pan.

Prick right through with a fork and press in blanched almonds at regular intervals.

Bake at 180 degrees C for 3/4 hour.

Sprinkle with castor sugar while warm.

Cut into fingers or squares.

Scotch Shortbread

Ingredients

250 ml sugar
250 ml butter
2 eggs
65 ml sour cream
625 ml flour
5 ml baking powder
5 ml grated lemon rind
Sliced, blanched almonds
Candied citrus peel
Little sugar

Method

Beat the butter until soft.

Gradually add the sugar and beat until creamy.

Beat in the eggs and the sour cream until very light and creamy.

Add the flour, baking powder and lemon rind.

Chill the dough for several hours.

Press the dough into 4 20.3 cm rounds.

Flute the edges and prick dough well.

Sprinkle the tops with almonds, candied peel and sugar.

Bake at 160 degrees C for 20 minutes.

Cut into wedges while still warm.

Shortbread

Ingredients

375 ml flour
130 ml margarine
25 ml castor sugar
Extra icing sugar

Method

Sift flour and rub in margarine.

Add sugar and mix until creamy.

Roll out to 5mm thickness.

Prick entire surface.

Cut into rounds.

Sprinkle with extra castor sugar.

Place on a baking sheet and bake at 160 degrees C for 20 minutes.

Dust with icing sugar.

Petticoat Tails

Ingredients

350 g flour
170 g butter
50 g sugar
4 tablespoons milk

Method

Mix together the flour and sugar.

Melt the butter and milk together.

Mix butter mixture into flour mixture.

Divide the dough into half.

Roll these halves out directly onto a baking tray into 9-inch round shapes.

Flute the edges.

Cut out a 2-inch circle from the centre but leave it in place.

Divide the outer ring into eight, keeping the inner circle whole.

Sprinkle with sugar.

Bake for 30 minutes at 180 degrees C.

Millionaires Shortbread

Ingredients

175 g butter
175 g sugar
225 g flour
60 g corn flour
1 teaspoon baking powder

Caramel

175 g sugar
175 g butter
450 g condensed milk
1 tablespoon syrup
Few drops of vanilla extract

Topping

175 g cark chocolate

Method

Make the Shortbread

Cream the butter and sugar together.
Add the flour, corn flour and baking powder.
Spread the mixture in a 30 cm baking tin.
Bake for 20 minutes at 180 degrees C.
Cool for 10 minutes.

Make the Caramel

Place all the ingredients except the vanilla into a saucepan.

Stir until the butter has melted and the sugar dissolved completely.

Boil for 5 to 7 minutes.

Add the vanilla and stir for 2 to 3 minutes.

Pour caramel over the shortbread.

Topping On The Caramel

Melt the chocolate over hot water.

Pour chocolate on caramel layer.

When shortbread has cooled down, cut into squares.

Butterscotch Shortbread

Ingredients

    125 ml butter
    125 ml shortening
    125 ml brown sugar
    75 ml sugar
    575 ml flour
    1 teaspoon salt

Method

Beat butter, shortening and sugar together.

Add flour and salt.

Roll dough and cut into 1 1/2 inch squares.

Place on an un-greased baking pan.

Bake for 25 minutes at 300 degrees F.

Ginger Shortbread

Ingredients

176 ml butter
83 ml icing sugar
3 tablespoons finely chopped crystallized ginger
333 ml flour
2 teaspoons sugar

Method

Beat the butter, icing sugar and ginger together.

Stir in the flour.

Pat the dough into a 9-inch circle on an un-greased baking sheet.

Sprinkle with sugar.

Bake for 20 minutes at 350 degrees F.

Cool for 10 minutes.

Cut the shortbread into wedges.

Cheddar Shortbread

Ingredients

250 ml flour
125 ml butter
5 ml salt
Pinch cayenne pepper
500 ml grated cheddar cheese

Topping

2 tablespoons poppy seeds
2 tablespoons sesame seeds
1 egg white
1 tablespoon water

Method

Mix flour, butter, salt and cayenne pepper together.

Add the cheese.

Shape dough into a circle and wrap in plastic food wrap.

Refrigerate 2 hours or overnight.

Roll out dough.

Cut with a cookie cutter into desired shapes.

Place onto an un-greased baking sheet.

Mix poppy seeds and sesame seeds together.

Beat the egg white and water together.

Brush shortbread cut outs with egg wash and sprinkle with seed mixture.

Bake for 12 minutes at 350 degrees F.

Chocolate Shortbread

Ingredients

315.5 ml flour
125 ml corn flour
10 tablespoons butter
65.5 ml icing sugar
2 tablespoons sugar
1/4 teaspoon salt
1/2 teaspoon vanilla extract
250 ml chocolate chips

Method

Mix flour and corn flour together.

Cream the butter until smooth.

Add the sugar, icing sugar, vanilla, and salt together.

Add butter mixture to flour mixture.

Knead in the chocolate chips.

Shape the dough into two equal parts, pat each into a 6 inch round, and transfer to baking sheet. Cut into wedges.

Bake for 25 minutes at 165 degrees C.

Allow shortbread to cool.

Melt remaining chips and drizzle over wedges.

Chocolate Chip Shortbread

Ingredients

250 ml butter
190.5 ml brown sugar
500 ml flour
250 ml chocolate chips

Method

Mix the butter and sugar together.

Add the flour and chocolate chips.

Roll the dough into balls.

Place the balls on an un-greased baking sheet.

Flatten the shortbread ball to about a 1/2-inch thickness with the greased bottom of a

glass, dipped in sugar.

Bake at 350 degrees F for 12 minutes.

Chocolate Dipped Shortbread

Ingredients

250 ml butter
125 ml sugar
500 ml cups flour
1 teaspoon vanilla extract
6 ounces chocolate chips

Method

Beat the butter and sugar together.

Add the flour and vanilla extract.

Toll dough into balls, roll in sugar and place on a baking sheet.

Flatten shortbread balls with a fork.

Bake for 12 minutes at 350 degrees F.

Cool shortbread for 10 minutes.

Melt the chocolate chips.

Dip half of each cookie into the melted chocolate.

Allow chocolate to set.

Lavender Shortbread

Ingredients

375 ml butter
166 ml sugar
2 tablespoons fresh lavender florets (very finely chopped)
1 tablespoon fresh mint (very finely chopped)
583 ml flour
125 ml corn flour
1.5 ml salt
Icing sugar to sprinkle on shortbread

Method

Beat the butter, sugar, lavender, and mint together.

Add the flour, corn flour, and salt to the butter mixture.

Wrap dough in plastic and chill until firm.

Rollout dough and cut into rounds.

Place on baking sheets.

Prick shortbread with a fork.

Bake for 20 minutes at 325 degrees F.

Sprinkle with icing sugar.

Honey Shortbread

Ingredients

375 ml butter
166 ml sugar
3 tablespoons honey
583 ml flour
125 ml corn flour
1.5 ml salt
Icing sugar to sprinkle on shortbread

Method

Beat the butter, sugar and honey together.
Add the flour, corn flour, and salt to the butter mixture.
Wrap dough in plastic and chill until firm.
Roll the dough out and cut into rounds.
Place on baking sheets.
Prick shortbread with a fork.
Bake for 20 minutes at 325 degrees F.
Sprinkle with icing sugar.

Coconut Shortbread

Ingredients

    250 ml butter
    62.5 ml sugar
    5 ml vanilla extract
    500 ml flour
    1 ml salt
    500 ml desiccated coconut
    250 ml icing sugar
    Icing sugar to sprinkle on shortbread

Method

Beat the butter and sugar together.

Add the flour, icing sugar, coconut, vanilla extract and salt to the butter mixture.

Wrap dough in plastic and chill until firm.

Roll the dough out and cut into rounds.

Place on baking sheets.

Prick shortbread with a fork.

Bake for 20 minutes at 325 degrees F.

Sprinkle with icing sugar.

Lemongrass Shortbread

Ingredients

375 ml butter
166 ml sugar
3 tablespoons lemongrass (mince very finely)
583 ml flour
125 ml corn flour
1.5 ml salt
Icing sugar to sprinkle on shortbread

Method

Beat the butter, sugar and lemongrass together.
Add the flour, corn flour, and salt to the butter mixture.
Wrap dough in plastic and chill until firm.
Rollout dough and cut into rounds.
Place on baking sheets.
Prick shortbread with a fork.
Bake for 20 minutes at 325 degrees F.
Sprinkle with icing sugar.

Cinnamon Shortbread

Ingredients

375 ml butter
166 ml brown sugar
10 ml cinnamon
583 ml flour
125 ml corn flour
1.5 ml salt
Icing sugar to sprinkle on shortbread

Method

Beat the butter, sugar together.

Add the flour, corn flour, cinnamon and salt to the butter mixture.

Wrap dough in plastic and chill until firm.

Rollout dough and cut into rounds.

Place on baking sheets.

Prick shortbread with a fork.

Bake for 20 minutes at 325 degrees F.

Sprinkle with icing sugar.

Rum And Raisin Shortbread

Ingredients

250 ml butter
62.5 ml sugar
5 ml vanilla extract
500 ml flour
1 ml salt
500 ml desiccated coconut
250 ml icing sugar
250 ml raisins
125 ml rum
Icing sugar to sprinkle on shortbread

Method

Beat the butter and sugar together.
Add the flour, vanilla extract, coconut, icing sugar and salt to the butter mixture.
Add the raisins and the rum.
Wrap dough in plastic and chill until firm.
Rollout dough and cut into rounds.
Place on baking sheets.
Prick shortbread with a fork.
Bake for 20 minutes at 325 degrees F.
Sprinkle with icing sugar.

Traditional Scottish Shortbread

Ingredients

500 g flour
500 g self-raising flour
500 g butter
225 g sugar
1 ml salt

Method

Beat the butter and sugar together.

Add the sieved flour and salt.

Shape into 2 rounds with your hands.

Place on a baking sheet.

Pinch the edges with your finger and thumb to give a nice finish.

Prick the base all over with a fork.

Bake for 60 minutes at 140 degrees C.

Whisky Chocolate Chip Shortbread

Ingredients

200 g flour
100 g corn flour
200 g butter
100 g icing sugar
100 g chocolate chips
3 tablespoons whisky
1 ml salt
Icing sugar to sprinkle on shortbread

Method

Beat the butter and icing sugar together.

Add the rest of the ingredients.

Mix to form dough.

Wrap dough in plastic and chill until firm.

Roll the dough out and cut into rounds.

Place on baking sheets.

Prick shortbread with a fork.

Bake for 20 minutes at 325 degrees F.

Sprinkle with icing sugar.

Whisky Pistachio Shortbread

Ingredients

200 g flour
100 g corn flour
200 g butter
100 g icing sugar
100 g pistachio nuts (shelled and chopped finely)
3 tablespoons whisky
1 ml salt
Icing sugar to sprinkle on shortbread

Method

Beat the butter and icing sugar together.

Add the rest of the ingredients.

Mix to form dough.

Wrap dough in plastic and chill until firm.

Roll the dough out and cut into rounds.

Place on baking sheets.

Prick shortbread with a fork.

Bake for 20 minutes at 325 degrees F.

Sprinkle with icing sugar.

Lemon Almond Shortbread

Ingredients

200 g flour
100 g corn flour
200 g butter
100 g icing sugar
100 g almond nuts (chopped finely)
3 tablespoons lemon juice
Zest of 1 lemon
1 ml salt
Icing sugar to sprinkle on shortbread

Method

Beat the butter and icing sugar together.
Add the rest of the ingredients.
Mix to form dough.
Wrap dough in plastic and chill until firm.
Roll the dough out and cut into rounds.
Place on baking sheets.
Prick shortbread with a fork.
Bake for 20 minutes at 325 degrees F.
Sprinkle with icing sugar.

White Chocolate And Macadamia Nut Shortbread

Ingredients

200 g flour
100 g corn flour
200 g butter
100 g icing sugar
100 g macadamia nuts (chopped finely)
100f white chocolate (broken into small pieces)
5 ml vanilla extract
1 ml salt
Icing sugar to sprinkle on shortbread

Method

Beat the butter and icing sugar together.

Add the rest of the ingredients.

Mix to form dough.

Wrap dough in plastic and chill until firm.

Roll the dough out and cut into rounds.

Place on baking sheets.

Prick shortbread with a fork.

Bake for 20 minutes at 325 degrees F.

Sprinkle with icing sugar.

Maple And Walnut Shortbread

Ingredients

200 g flour
100 g corn flour
200 g butter
100 g icing sugar
100 g walnuts (shelled and chopped finely)
3 tablespoons maple syrup
1 ml salt
Icing sugar to sprinkle on shortbread

Method

Beat the butter and icing sugar together.

Add the rest of the ingredients.

Mix to form dough.

Wrap dough in plastic and chill until firm.

Roll the dough out and cut into rounds.

Place on baking sheets.

Prick shortbread with a fork.

Bake for 20 minutes at 325 degrees F.

Sprinkle with icing sugar.

Rosemary And Walnut Shortbread

Ingredients

200 g flour
100 g corn flour
200 g butter
100 g icing sugar
100 g walnuts (shelled and chopped finely)
3 tablespoons crushed dried rosemary
1 ml salt
Icing sugar to sprinkle on shortbread

Method

Beat the butter and icing sugar together.

Add the rest of the ingredients.

Mix to form dough.

Wrap dough in plastic and chill until firm.

Roll the dough out and cut into rounds.

Place on baking sheets.

Prick shortbread with a fork.

Bake for 20 minutes at 325 degrees F.

Sprinkle with icing sugar.

White Chocolate And Cherry Shortbread

Ingredients

375 ml flour
130 ml butter
25 ml castor sugar
White chocolate (melted)
125 ml Maraschino cherries (chopped)

Method

Sift flour and rub in margarine.

Add sugar and mix until creamy.

Add the cherries.

Roll out to 5mm thickness.

Prick entire surface.

Cut into rounds.

Sprinkle with extra castor sugar.

Place on a baking sheet and bake at 160 degrees C for 20 minutes.

Dip half the shortbread cookie in the melted white chocolate.

Allow the chocolate to set.

Lemon Verbena Shortbread

Ingredients

    375 ml flour
    130 ml butter
    25 ml castor sugar
    125 ml lemon Verbena leaves

Method

Put Lemon Verbena leaves into a blender and blend until very fine.

Sift flour and rub in margarine.

Add sugar and mix until creamy.

Add the cherries.

Roll out to 5mm thickness.

Prick entire surface.

Cut into rounds.

Sprinkle with extra castor sugar.

Place on a baking sheet and bake at 160 degrees C for 20 minutes.

Dip half the shortbread cookie in the melted white chocolate.

Allow the chocolate to set.

Espresso And Dark Chocolate Shortbread

Ingredients

200 g flour
100 g corn flour
200 g butter
100 g icing sugar
1 1/2 tablespoons espresso powder
1/4 cup espresso beans (roughly ground)
1 ml salt
Dark chocolate (melted)

Method

Beat the butter and icing sugar together.

Add the rest of the ingredients (except for the espresso beans).

Mix to form dough.

Wrap dough in plastic and chill until firm.

Sprinkle the ground espresso beans in the bottom of the pan.

Press the dough into a baking pan (make sure it is pressed down firmly).

Prick the shortbread all over with a fork.

Bake for 20 minutes at 325 degrees F.

Let cool for 10 minutes and cut into fingers.

Dip one side of each finger into the melted chocolate.

Mocha Shortbread

Ingredients

    312.5 ml flour
    62.5 ml corn flour
    62.5 ml cocoa powder
    4 ml instant coffee powder
    1 ml salt
    250 ml butter
    250 ml icing sugar
    3 oz white chocolate (melted)
    3 oz bittersweet dark chocolate (melted)

Method

Beat the butter and icing sugar together.

Add the rest of the ingredients (except the chocolate).

Mix to form dough.

Wrap dough in plastic and chill until firm.

Press the dough into a baking pan (make sure it is pressed down firmly).

Prick the shortbread all over with a fork.

Bake for 20 minutes at 325 degrees F.

Let cool for 10 minutes and cut into fingers.

Dip one end of the finger into the white melted chocolate.

Let the chocolate set.

Dip the other end in the dark chocolate.

Let the chocolate set.

Cranberry Brandy Shortbread

Ingredients

    200 g flour
    100 g corn flour
    200 g butter
    100 g icing sugar
    100 g cranberries
    3 tablespoons brandy
    1 ml salt
    White chocolate (melted)

Method

Beat the butter and icing sugar together.

Add the rest of the ingredients.

Mix to form dough.

Wrap dough in plastic and chill until firm.

Roll the dough out and cut into rounds.

Place on baking sheets.

Prick shortbread with a fork.

Bake for 20 minutes at 325 degrees F.

Dip one end of cookie into the melted white chocolate.

Allow chocolate to set.

Lemon Honey Shortbread

Ingredients

200 g flour
100 g corn flour
200 g butter
100 g icing sugar
1 tablespoon grated lemon zest
3 tablespoons honey
1 ml salt

Lemon Glace Icing

125 ml icing sugar
15 ml lemon juice
25 ml butter

Method

Beat the butter and icing sugar together.

Add the rest of the ingredients.

Mix to form dough.

Wrap dough in plastic and chill until firm.

Roll the dough out and cut into rounds.

Place on baking sheets.

Prick shortbread with a fork.

Bake for 20 minutes at 325 degrees F.

Make the glace icing by adding the icing sugar to the butter and the lemon juice.

Mix until smooth.

Ice the top of each shortbread cookie with the glace icing.

Chai Shortbread

Ingredients

  200 g flour
  100 g corn flour
  200 g butter
  100 g icing sugar
  1 ml salt
  5 ml vanilla extract
  7.5 ml Chai tealeaves
  3 ml ground cinnamon

Method

Beat the butter and icing sugar together.

Add the rest of the ingredients.

Mix to form dough.

Wrap dough in plastic and chill until firm.

Press the dough into a baking pan (make sure it is pressed down firmly).

Prick the shortbread all over with a fork.

Bake for 20 minutes at 325 degrees F.

Let cool for 10 minutes and cut into fingers.

Nougat Shortbread

Ingredients

200 g flour
100 g corn flour
200 g butter
100 g icing sugar
1 ml salt
500 g Nougat bar (frozen and chopped into pieces)

Method

Beat the butter and icing sugar together.

Add the rest of the ingredients.

Mix to form dough.

Wrap dough in plastic and chill until firm.

Press the dough into a baking pan (make sure it is pressed down firmly).

Prick the shortbread all over with a fork.

Bake for 20 minutes at 325 degrees F.

Let cool for 10 minutes and cut into fingers.

Chocolate Rose Shortbread

Ingredients

200 g flour
100 g corn flour
200 g butter
100 g icing sugar
1 ml salt
5 ml rose water
25 ml crushed, dried rose petals
White chocolate (melted)
Additional crushed, dried rose petals to decorate shortbread cookies

Method

Beat the butter and icing sugar together.

Add the rest of the ingredients.

Mix to form dough.

Wrap dough in plastic and chill until firm.

Press the dough into a baking pan (make sure it is pressed down firmly).

Prick the shortbread all over with a fork.

Bake for 20 minutes at 325 degrees F.

Let cool for 10 minutes and cut into fingers.

Dip one half of the shortbread cookie into the melted chocolate.

Sprinkle the crushed, dried rose petals onto the chocolate.

Allow chocolate to set.

Blue Cheese And Fig Shortbread

Ingredients

    250 ml flour
    125 ml butter
    5 ml salt
    3 ml ground black pepper
    250 ml crumbled blue cheese
    250 ml dried figs, chopped into small pieces

Method

Mix flour, butter, salt and black pepper together.

Add the cheese and dried figs.

Shape dough into a circle and wrap in plastic food wrap.

Refrigerate 2 hours or overnight.

Roll out dough.

Cut with a cookie cutter into desired shapes.

Place onto an un-greased baking sheet.

Bake for 12 to 15 minutes at 350 degrees F.

Fig And Ginger Shortbread

Ingredients

    250 ml butter
    125 ml brown sugar
    625 ml flour
    125 ml crystallized ginger, cut into small pieces
    250 ml dried figs, cut into small pieces
    3 ml ground cinnamon
    1 ml salt

Method

Mix the butter and sugar together.

Beat in the flour and cinnamon and mix thoroughly.

Add the ginger and the figs.

Chill the dough.

Shape into 2.5 cm balls and place on an un-greased baking sheet.

Press a criss-cross design on top of each ball with a floured fork.

Bake at 150 degree C for 20 minutes. The tops should not be brown.

Chili Chocolate Shortbread

Ingredients

    312.5 ml flour
    62.5 ml corn flour
    62.5 ml cocoa powder
    4 ml dried, crushed chili peppers
    1ml salt
    250 ml butter
    250 ml icing sugar
    Dark Chocolate (melted)

Method

Beat the butter and icing sugar together.

Add the rest of the ingredients.

Mix to form dough.

Wrap dough in plastic and chill until firm.

Press the dough into a baking pan (make sure it is pressed down firmly).

Prick the shortbread all over with a fork.

Bake for 20 minutes at 325 degrees F.

Let cool for 10 minutes and cut into fingers.

Dip one end of the finger into the dark melted chocolate.

Let the chocolate set.

Dip the other end in the dark chocolate.

Let the chocolate set.

Strawberry And Cracked Black Pepper Shortbread

Ingredients

500 ml flour
245 ml margarine
190 ml icing sugar
125 ml corn flour
250 ml strawberries, chopped into small pieces
7.5 ml ground fresh black pepper

Method

Beat the margarine and icing sugar until creamy.

Beat in the flour and corn flour.

Add strawberries and black pepper.

Drop teaspoons onto a greased baking tray.

Bake at 160 degrees C until lightly brown.

Pecan And Cranberry Chocolate Shortbread

Ingredients

    160 ml icing sugar
    245 ml butter
    5 ml vanilla essence
    500 ml flour
    125 ml pecan nuts
    125 ml dried cranberries
    Dark Chocolate (melted)

Method

Beat the margarine and the icing sugar until creamy.

Add the rest of the ingredients.

Roll out to a 9mm thickness, cut with 3 cm round cutter.

Place on a baking sheet.

Bake at 160 degrees C until starting to brown (do not allow to brown).

Dip one side of the shortbread cookies in the melted dark chocolate.

Allow the chocolate to set.

Amaretto And Cherry Shortbread

Ingredients

375 ml flour
130 ml butter
25 ml castor sugar
125 ml dried cherries (chopped into pieces)
3 tablespoons Amaretto

Method

Sift flour and rub in margarine.

Add sugar and mix until creamy.

Add the cherries and the Amaretto.

Roll out to 5mm thickness.

Prick entire surface.

Cut into rounds.

Sprinkle with extra castor sugar.

Place on a baking sheet and bake at 160 degrees C for 20 minutes.

Allow shortbread to cool for 10 minutes.

Vanilla And Saffron Shortbread

Ingredients

200 g flour
100 g corn flour
200 g butter
100 g icing sugar
1 ml salt
12.5 ml vanilla extract
5 ml saffron
White chocolate (melted)
Additional saffron to decorate cookie

Method

Beat the butter and icing sugar together.

Add the rest of the ingredients.

Mix to form dough.

Wrap dough in plastic and chill until firm.

Press the dough into a baking pan (make sure it is pressed down firmly).

Prick the shortbread all over with a fork.

Bake for 20 minutes at 325 degrees F.

Let cool for 10 minutes and cut into fingers.

Drizzle the shortbread cookie with melted chocolate.

Sprinkle saffron on unset chocolate.

Allow chocolate to set.

Cardamom And Rose Shortbread

Ingredients

200 g flour
100 g corn flour
200 g butter
100 g icing sugar
100 g almond nuts (chopped finely)
1 ml salt
7.5 ml ground cardamom
5 ml rose water
White chocolate (melted)

Method

Beat the butter and icing sugar together.

Add the rest of the ingredients.

Mix to form dough.

Wrap dough in plastic and chill until firm.

Roll the dough out and cut into rounds.

Place on baking sheets.

Prick shortbread with a fork.

Bake for 20 minutes at 325 degrees F.

Drizzle with melted white chocolate

Cardamom And Pistachio Shortbread

Ingredients

200 g flour
100 g corn flour
200 g butter
100 g icing sugar
100 g pistachio nuts (shelled and chopped finely)
5 ml ground cardamom
1 ml salt
Icing sugar to sprinkle on shortbread

Method

Beat the butter and icing sugar together.

Add the rest of the ingredients.

Mix to form dough.

Wrap dough in plastic and chill until firm.

Roll the dough out and cut into rounds.

Place on baking sheets.

Prick shortbread with a fork.

Bake for 20 minutes at 325 degrees F.

Sprinkle with icing sugar.

Apricot And Walnut Shortbread

Ingredients

250 ml butter
125 ml brown sugar
625 ml flour
375 ml dried apricot, cut into small pieces
250 ml walnuts, chopped into small pieces
1 ml salt
Icing sugar to sprinkle on baked cookies

Method

Mix the butter and sugar together.

Beat in the flour and mix thoroughly.

Add the apricots and the walnuts.

Chill the dough.

Shape into 2.5 cm balls and place on an un-greased baking sheet.

Press a criss-cross design on top of each ball with a floured fork.

Bake at 150 degree C for 20 minutes. The tops should not be brown.

Allow the shortbread to cool for 10 minutes.

Sprinkle icing sugar on shortbread.

Coffee Liqueur And Hazelnut Shortbread

Ingredients

250 ml butter
125 ml brown sugar
625 ml flour
3 tablespoons coffee liqueur
250 ml hazelnuts, chopped into small pieces
3 ml ground cinnamon
1 ml salt
Dark chocolate (melted)

Method

Mix the butter and sugar together.

Beat in the flour and cinnamon and mix thoroughly.

Add the hazelnuts and the coffee liqueur.

Chill the dough.

Shape into 2.5 cm balls and place on an un-greased baking sheet.

Press a criss-cross design on top of each ball with a floured fork.

Bake at 150 degree C for 20 minutes. The tops should not be brown.

Allow the shortbread to cool for 10 minutes.

Drizzle the shortbread with melted dark chocolate.

Allow the chocolate to set.

Made in the USA
San Bernardino, CA
03 August 2015